DO YOU LIKE BIG GIRLS? 7
story & art by Goro Aizome

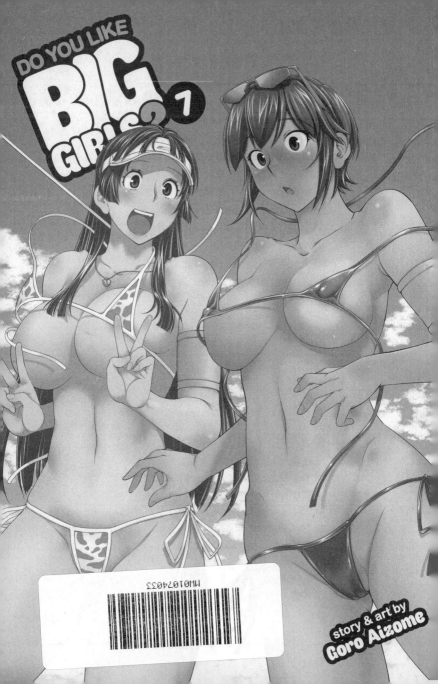

Recap

Tachibana Sota was roped into becoming the coach for his sister's all-girl college volleyball team and the hall director for their dormitory. Being so short and the only boy around, he's naturally the perfect target for these voluptuous amazons' tantalizing teasing and sexual advances. What surprises await Sota as he attempts to navigate the titillating twists and turns of dorm life?

7

C O N T E N T S

Attack No. 59 **Operation: Beauty Pageant**   3

Attack No. 60 **The Formula for Victory**   13

Attack No. 61 **S Is for "I'm Sorry"**   25

Attack No. 62 **The Space between Chastity and Lust**   41

Attack No. 63 **The Handbook of a Horny Slut**   59

Attack No. 64 **Pride and Marshmallows**   75

Attack No. 65 **Say My Name**   93

Attack No. 66 **If Only My Tears Made Me Stronger**   111

Attack No. 67 **Unforgettable...**   129

IT ALREADY FEELS LIKE FALL!
Sapporo Autumn Festival 2019
9/6 (Fri) ~ 9/29 (Sun) 10 a.m. ~ 8:30 p.m. Last Order 8 p.m.
NORTH
MISO RAMEN
I SWEAR SUMMER BOOT CAMP WAS ONLY YESTERDAY.
WE REALLY TRAINED HARD! ☆
MEANING IT'S ALMOST TIME FOR THE FALL TOURNAMENT!
THE HOKUEI FESTIVAL COMES FIRST, NEECHAN.
Aaah!
Giants!
SHUFFLE
MUNCH MUNCH
SHUFFLE
They're so tall!
Sure are.
HRM.
ARE WE DOING THE TAKOYAKI CART AGAIN?
I CAN'T WAIT!

Attack No. 59
Operation: Beauty Pageant

LET'S GIVE THAT TOURNAMENT EVERYTHING WE'VE GOT!
THERE'S OUR ACE!
BONK
Oof!

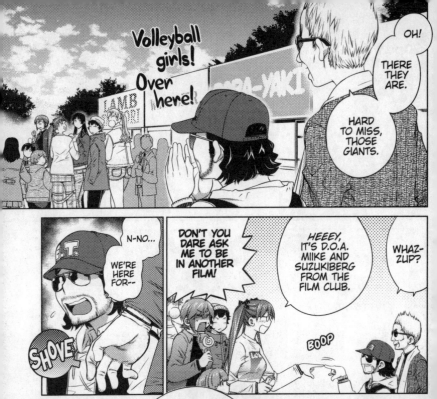

Volleyball girls! Over here!

OH!

THERE THEY ARE.

HARD TO MISS, THOSE GIANTS.

N-NO... WE'RE HERE FOR--

DON'T YOU DARE ASK ME TO BE IN ANOTHER FILM!

HEEEY, IT'S D.O.A. MIIKE AND SUZUKIBERG FROM THE FILM CLUB.

WHAZZUP?

SHOVE!

BOOP

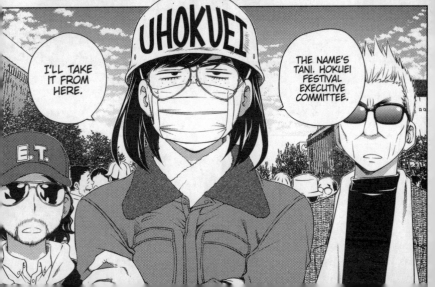

UHOKUEI

I'LL TAKE IT FROM HERE.

THE NAME'S TANI. HOKUEI FESTIVAL EXECUTIVE COMMITTEE.

E.T.

Student Council
A B...
BEAUTY PAGEANT?!
FOR THE SPORTS TEAMS?!
YES.
MUNCH MUNCH
Blah
THE COMMITTEE IS CONCERNED ABOUT THE RECENT DECLINE IN HOKUEI FESTIVAL ATTENDANCE.
TO COUNTERACT THIS, WE WANT TO PUT MORE EMPHASIS ON THE SPORTS TEAMS...
Blah
Blah
Blah
WE'RE LOOKING FOR THREE VOLUNTEERS FROM EACH TEAM TO PARTICIPATE.
WE'D BE GLAD TO--
BONK
HELP?!
FORGET IT! WE'RE DOING OUR TAKOYAKI STAND AND THAT'S ALL!
THE WINNER GETS 300,000 YEN.
Blah blah blah blah and--
Oof!

THREE--?!
A THOUSAND TIMES YES!
SHOVE
MUNCH
MUNCH
OH GOD...
SHE'S PROBABLY PICTURING ALL THE KINKY TOYS SHE'LL BUY...
TINGLE
AND WHAT DO PARTICIPANTS GET?
UH...
LET'S SEE... T-TEN...
F...
FIVE THOU-SAND YEN!
MUNCH
MUNCH
WE'LL DO IT!
SO...
WHAT'S IN IT FOR THE FILM CLUB?
GLANCE
NOTH-ING!
WE JUST --!

WE WERE PLANNING ON *MAYBE* SHOOTING SOME FOOTAGE OF THE EVENT...
WHAT?! YOU WERE GONNA *SELL US OUT?!*
OUR CLUB'S GOT ITS OWN MONEY ISSUES, Y'KNOW...
FWIP
......
?
MUNCH
MUNCH
TWO? TWENTY THOU-SAND?
SURELY YOU JEST.
TWO PERCENT...
OF YOUR TOTAL SALES.
THIS DEAL'S JUST BETWEEN US AND THE FILM CLUB.
THE COMMITTEE DOESN'T HAVE TO GET INVOLVED.
SO, WHAT DO YOU SAY?
DEAL.
Whaaa?!

Hokuei College
Girls' Dorm
Suzuka Villa
YOU'RE ONE SHREWD BUSINESS-WOMAN, CAP!
LOOK.
EQUIPMENT AND TRAVEL...
ALL THOSE THINGS COST MONEY, RIGHT?
THAT GRAND PRIZE WILL BE PRETTY SWEET, TOO.
HUH? YOU THINK WE CAN WIN?
PROB-ABLY.
HOW'S THAT, EXACTLY?
YOU GOT A PLAN?
SLURP
WELL.
MAY-BE...

THE MAIN ISSUE IS THE ROSTER.
WHO'S GONNA JOIN THE BIRDBRAIN BIMBOS?
JULIA MCKENZIE: CONFIRMED
HASEGAWA AYANO: CONFIRMED
Yaaay!♥
イェーイ
Weee!♥
わーい
ばっ
Yes!
DON'T LOOK AT ME. I'M DOUBLE-BOOKED WITH THE TAKOYAKI STAND AND THE MANGA CLUB.
ASAKURA SAKURA: DECLINED
UH.
THAT'S A HARD PASS FROM ME.
NUNOURA SUZUNA: DECLINED
I'LL TOTALLY DO IT!
ムキ FLEX
ムキ FLEX
NONOURA NAZUNA: WILLING
I MEAN... I'M F-FINE WITH IT...
But I'm flat as a board.
TESHIGAWARA KYOKA: WILLING-ISH
I'M T-TERRIFIED OF MEN...
ブルブル
SHAKE SHAKE
GOOD POINT...
FUJIWARA RURI: DECLINED

WHAT ABOUT YOU, CAPTAIN?
ME?!
I'M A CHONK MONSTER!
KARA-AGE!
KARA-AGE!
SHE'S...
NOT WRONG...
YAMADA SANAE: CHONK MONSTER
THEN THAT LEAVES NEECHAN.
SHE'S OUR ONLY OTHER OPTION...
BUT SHE'S PRETTY ENOUGH TO WIN.
Grrooowwl...
Grrr... Grrrr...
SPEAKING OF KAORU, WHERE IS SHE?
OH.
TAKING A BATH.
Yep.
Karaage!

FWOOOSH
TACHIBANA KAORU: MID-SHOWER
PHEW!
KA-CHAK
OH. HERE SHE IS.
SCARY SUMMIT
HUH? YOU STILL NEED ONE MORE VOLUNTEER?
PASS!
WE ALREADY DECIDED YOU'RE IN.
WHUH?!
ROCK-PAPER-SCISSORS!
ARRRRGH!
Paper
TACHIBANA KAORU: CONFIRMED, PISSED

LET'S GET GRILLING.
PEEK
OKAY.
Attack No. 60
The Formula for Victory
Takoyaki
Café
SIZZZLE
RICE BALL
FRIED PORK
じゅうぅぅ
SIZZZZZLE
96th Annual
HOKUEI FESTIVAL
Sponsored by the Hokuei College Student Council
Hokuei College Entrance
OOOH!

OKAY, EVERYONE! IT'S TIME TO BEGIN...
THE HOKUEI BEAUTY PAGEANT, FEATURING OUR TOP FEMALE ATHLETES!
LET'S HAVE A ROUND OF APPLAUSE FOR THE SWIM TEAM!

NEXT UP, IT'S THE SOFTBALL TEAM!
FOLLOWED BY THE WOMEN'S BASKETBALL TEAM!
THE... UH... WOMEN'S KENDO TEAM...
HOKUEI TANAKA
NOT MUCH OF A SHOW.
THE SWIM TEAM'S GOT THIS.
'Cause of the swimsuits.
SHUT UP AND KEEP FILMING.
LAST BUT NOT LEAST!
PRESENT-ING THE WOMEN'S VOLLEY-BALL TEAM!

WHOOOOOOO!
OOOO!

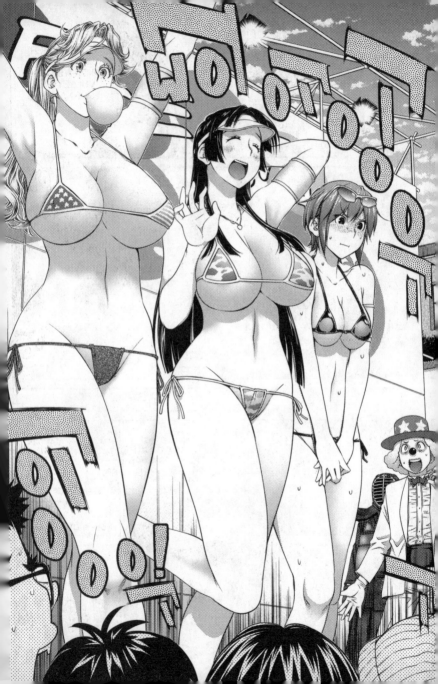

THIS SUMMER, THE TEAM WON A BEACH VOLLEYBALL TOURNAMENT...
OOO
OOO
OOO
HENCE THE BIKINIS!
OOOO
OOOH!
WOO
SO THIS WAS YOUR SECRET WEAPON, HUH?
OOO!
Nee-hee.
WOO
HEY! THAT'S PLAYING DIRTY!
OH.
HI, CAPTAIN OF THE TEAM THAT LOST TO US TWICE!
WOO!
SH-SHUT UP!
Bwa ha ha!
IN THE END, MESSING WITH THEIR TEAM WAS ALL WE REALLY DID AT BOOT CAMP.
YEP...
......

MISAKA
SHWF
WHAM!
YEAAAAAAAH!
PUMP.

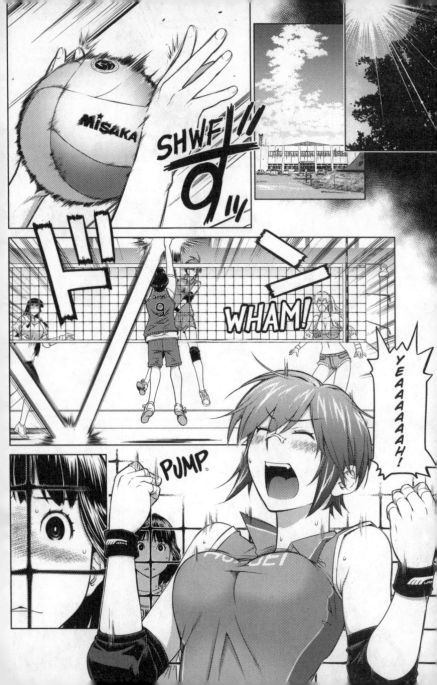

L...
LET'S PLAY SOME BALL!
だむっ
DUNK
HOKUEI
9

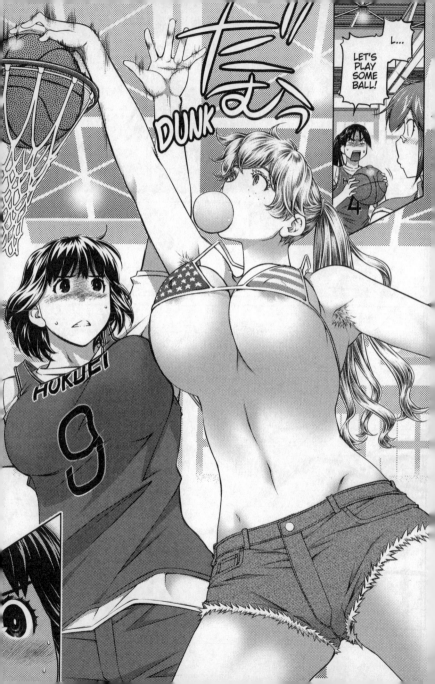

SO TELL US, WHAT MOVES ARE YOU LOVELY LADIES BEST AT?
UH... I'M GOOD AT...
SHOVE
HOKUEI
SPIKING...
HOKUEI
SWIPE
BOING

EEK!
FREEDOM!
WOOO!♥
SHOOF
JIGGLE

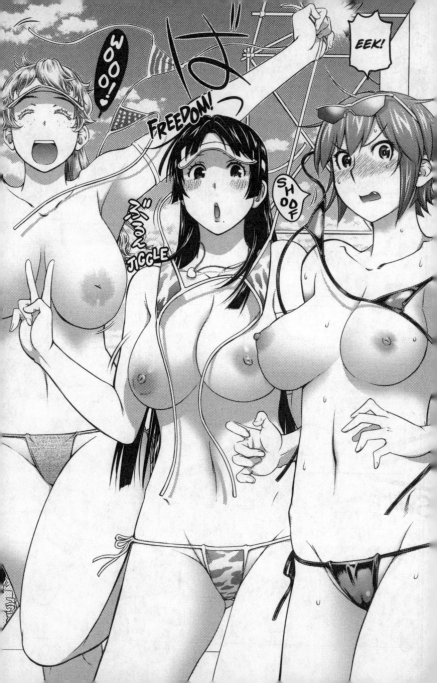

Takoyaki
10 FOR 500
HOLY HELL.
THE CROWD AT THE BEAUTY PAGEANT IS REALLY GOING WILD.
IN THE END...
DUE TO LEWD AND DISORDERLY CONDUCT, THE VOLLEYBALL TEAM WAS DISQUALIFIED...
AND BANNED FROM ALL CLUB ACTIVITIES.
MEANING THEY COULDN'T PLAY IN THE FALL TOURNAMENT AFTER ALL...
Crêpe
STAGE

DO YOU LIKE BIG GIRLS?

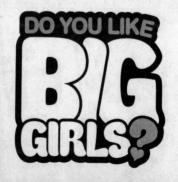

DO YOU LIKE BIG GIRLS?

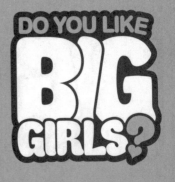

Attack No. 61
S Is for "I'm Sorry"
SQUEAK
ACK!
IT'S THE BASKETBALL TEAM THAT LOST TO US TWELVE TIMES IN A ROW!
You kept score?!
WILL YOU QUIT THAT?!
LOOK...
THE REASON WE'RE HERE IS...

STAGE
WE CAME TO APOLOGIZE FOR ALL THE TROUBLE THIS BRAT CAUSED.
GO ON.
SAY YOU'RE SORRY.
WHAT?
HURRY UP.
THIS IS AWK-WARD.
WHY SHOULD I? HAIRY ARMPIT GIRL TOOK HER BIKINI TOP OFF ALL BY HERSELF!
AND AYANO-SENPAI'S TOP.
Hairy Armpit Girl?
It's truuue!♡
I regret nothing!
It is apt...
AND WHO'S THIS BABY PIGLET?
A TEENSY TWINKIE?
I'M THE CAPTAIN!
Not dinner!
REGARDLESS, YOU'RE THE ONE WHO SET OFF THAT CHAIN REACTION, RIGHT?
......

WHAT ABOUT HER? SHE DIDN'T SEEM UPSET THAT I RIPPED HER TOP OFF.
WHA ?!
H-HOW DARE YOU!
I'M UPSET! I'M VERY UPSET!
CALM DOWN.
HOW ABOUT A COMPRO-MISE?
WHAT DO YOU THINK ABOUT...
JOINING OUR TEAM?
EW, NO.
DON'T BE SO HASTY...
I'D DO ANYTHING TO HAVE A FORMER STAR PLAYER ON OUR TEAM...

HOW ABOUT YOU COME PRACTICE WITH US SOMETIMES?
NO.
JUST COME TO MATCHES?
STOP.
You're from Miyagi, right?
HRM.
SQUEAK
WHAT IF...
I THREW IN A NICE BOOB MASSAGE TO--

WHAT THE HELL, SOTA?!!
IT'D BE LIKE...
KILLING TWO BIRDS WITH ONE STONE, RIGHT?
I'LL SHOW YOU KILL-ING!!
AND KNOCK IT OFF WITH THE PERVY EYES!
THEY'RE CALLED "BEDROOM EYES," NEECHAN.
THEY'LL BE HOSPITALIZED EYES IF YOU DON'T--
Tee hee.
I'M IN. BOOBS AND ALL.
HUH?!
WHAT?!

THEY'RE ALL YOURS. ♡
ぽよん
BOING
I...
I CAN'T...
HUH?
IF THEY'RE NOT NAKED...
I DON'T WANT 'EM!!
くわっ
RAWR!

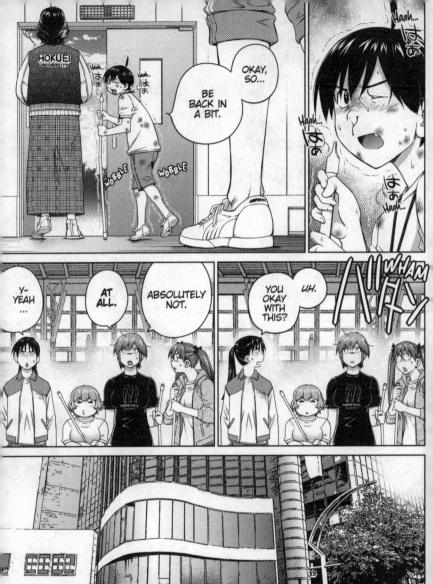

OKAY, SO...

BE BACK IN A BIT.

Haah... はあ

Haah... はあ

HOKUEI UNIVERSITY

WOBBLE WOBBLE

Haah... はあ

Haah... はあ

はあ

Haah...

Y-YEAH...

AT ALL.

ABSOLUTELY NOT.

YOU OKAY WITH THIS?

UH.

WHAM ハッ

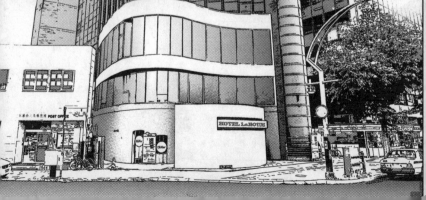

HOTEL LaBOUR

FWOOOOOOOOSH
WIPE
WIPE
YANK
NOW THEN! ♡ IF YOU'LL DO THE HONORS...

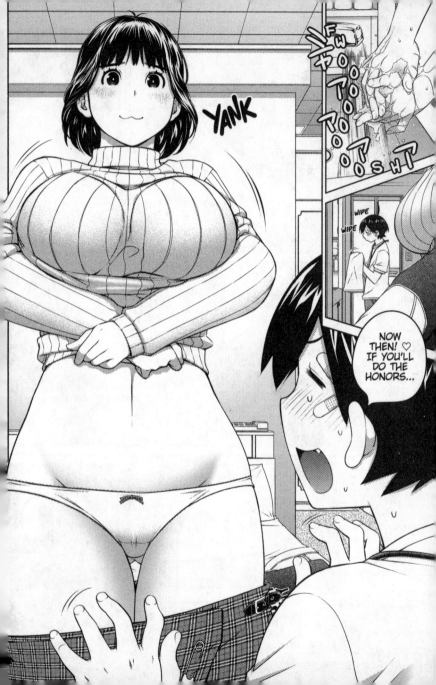

ばいん
SPROING
PRE...
TTY...
GRAB
PLEASE!

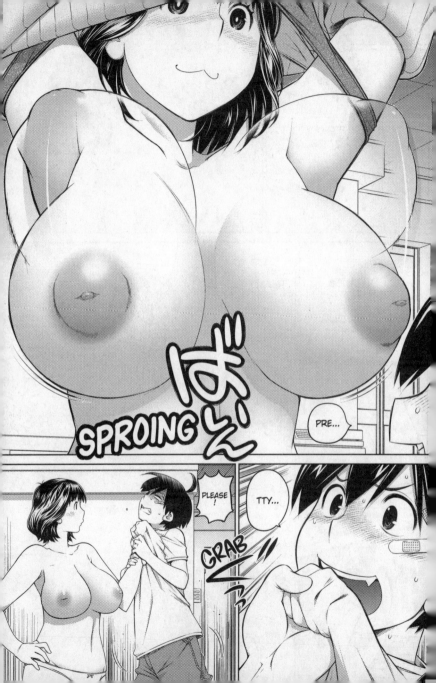

WHAT WAS YOUR NAME AGAIN?
S- SOTA...
TACHIBANA SOTA...
WELL... SOTA-KUN.
ROLL
DID YOU THINK I WAS REALLY GONNA LET YOU FONDLE MY BOOBS?
JIGGLE
HUH?
I ONLY SAID YES BECAUSE I KNEW IT WOULD ROYALLY PISS OFF YOUR SISTER.

うる
WIBBLE
うる
WIBBLE
You're crying?
Sigh...
CRAB
FINE.
NOW WE'RE EVEN.
SQUISH
AND WITH THAT, I'M OUT OF HERE.
CREAK
SEE YA 'ROUND... SHORTCAKE, WAS IT?
SMIRK

SQUEAK
SQUEAK
SQUEAK
THAT GIRL'S GOT A MOUTH ON HER.
SORRY ABOUT THAT...
SHE CALLED ME A TWINKIE!
SQUEAK
SQUEAK
UH-OH...
MY SHORTCAKE SENSE IS TINGLING...
HRM?
ALLOW ME TO EXPLAIN!

THANKS TO KAORU'S CHILDHOOD MEDDLING, SOTA BECOMES A RAGING BEAST...
WHENEVER ANYONE CALLS HIM "SHORTCAKE"!
Huff! Huff! Huff! Huff!
LICK LICK LICK LICK LICK LICK
JUST NOT A VERY STRONG ONE.
HISSSSSS!
LICK LICK LICK LICK
KICK KICK KICK
......
GULP
ROLL
SO--
LICK LICK LICK LICK
THROB
SO ROUGH!
THROB
LICK LICK LICK LICK
SHOOP
SHOOP

AAAH!
LICK LICK LICK LICK
LICK LICK LICK LICK
LICK LICK LICK LICK
GROPE GROPE
AAAAA-AAAH! ♡
SO.
I PUT TOGETHER A MAKE-OUT SCHEDULE.
WHAT'S A MAKE-OUT SCHEDULE?
MUNCH MUNCH
ARE YOU FEELING ALL RIGHT?
Ahem.

HASEGAWA AYANO
SUN
YAMADA SANAE
MON
TESHIGAWARA KYOKA
TUES
JULIA MCKENZIE
WED
ASAKURA SAKURA
THURS
NUNOURA NAZUNA
FRI
FUJIWARA RURI
SAT
THIS...
FAIRLY ALLOWS YOU EACH TO GET A PIECE OF SOTA-KUN.
YOU JUST DON'T GET IT, SUZUNA-TAN.
YOU CAN'T SCHEDULE THAT-- IT'S ALL ABOUT BEING IN THE RIGHT MOOD.
Sigh...
MUNCH
MUNCH
WHAM
SHUT IT!
WHAT ABOUT KAORU'S TURN?
カチャ
KA-CHAK
WHAT ABOUT YOU?
ME?
I DON'T NEED A TURN.

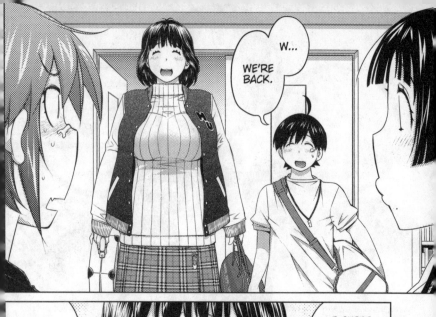

W... WE'RE BACK.

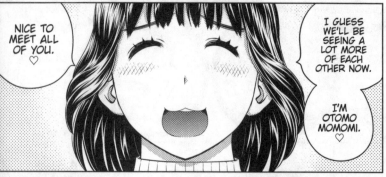

NICE TO MEET ALL OF YOU. ♡

I GUESS WE'LL BE SEEING A LOT MORE OF EACH OTHER NOW.

I'M OTOMO MOMOMI. ♡

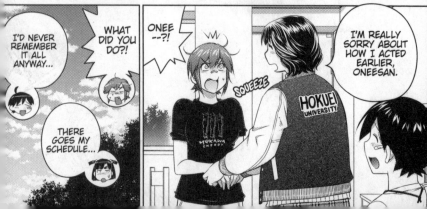

I'D NEVER REMEMBER IT ALL ANYWAY...

WHAT DID YOU DO?!

ONEE--?!

THERE GOES MY SCHEDULE...

SQUEEZE

HOKUEI UNIVERSITY

I'M REALLY SORRY ABOUT HOW I ACTED EARLIER, ONEESAN.

Aah!♡
Aah!♡
Aah!♡
Haah...
Haah...
Haah...
CREAK
CREAK
CREAK

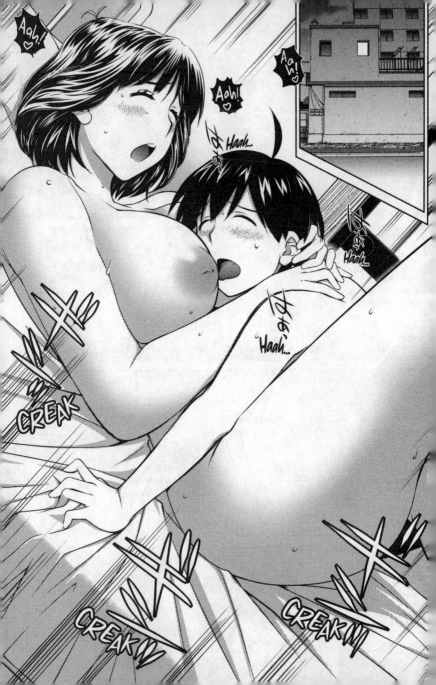

Aah!♡
CREAK
Aah!♡
CREAK
Aah!♡
CREAK
Aah!♡
Aah!♡
CREAK!!!
Aah!♡
CREAK!!!
......
Aah!♡♡
AYANO...
WE NEED TO TALK.
KA-CHAK
Oh!♡
Yeah!♡
Oh yeah!♡
I'm cumming!♡
AYANO!
WE NEED TO TALK!
Yes!♡
?

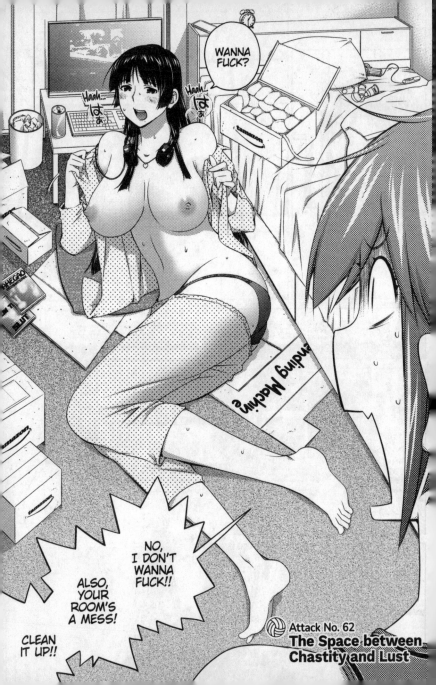

Attack No. 62
The Space between
Chastity and Lust

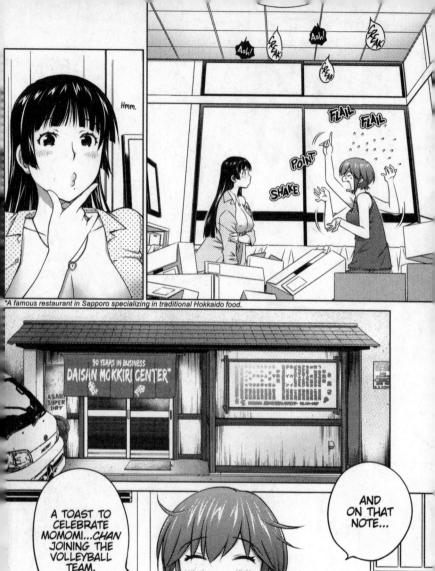

*A famous restaurant in Sapporo specializing in traditional Hokkaido food.

CHEEERS !!!
DRINK! DRINK!
COME ON, SOTA! DRINK UP!
CHUG
CHUG
Fwah!
SNOOORE...
SSNOOORRE...

SNOOORE...
ぐおぉ
キィ...
CLACK
IS HE ASLEEP?
YEAH... OUT LIKE A LIGHT.
SNAP
SNAP
CLINK
HUH?
CLINK
W DOES S THING ORK?
CLINK
SLIDE IT IN HERE...
CLINK
HUH?
CLINK
INK

UH.
SHFF
CRAP, HE WOKE UP.
POP
CLICK
HRM?

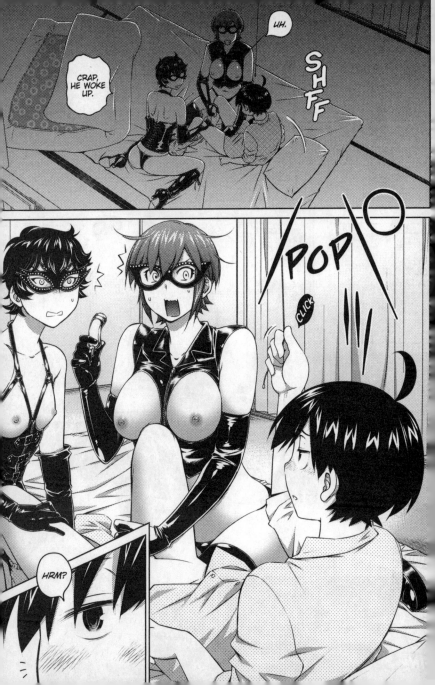

A CHASTITY BELT.
CLINK
A DEVICE THAT'S LOCKED IN PLACE OVER THE GENITALIA TO PREVENT SEXUAL INTERCOURSE.
FWUMP
WHAT IS THAT?
WHAT ARE YOU TWO DOING?
IT'S...
A CHASTITY BELT...
WE WERE TRYING TO GET IT ON YOU...
I THOUGHT YOU WERE INTO STUFF LIKE THIS?!
I JUST LIKE THE AES-THETIC!
IT'S FINE.
PUT IT ON.
SERI-OUSLY?!
IT'S KINDA COOL!
LIKE I'M A MECHA.
Y-YEAH! TOTALLY MECHA-ESQUE!
CLINK
CLINK
CLINK

Ta-daaa!
CLINK
CLINK
WHOA!
I FEEL STRONGER ALREADY!
YOU'RE *SO* STRONG, MECHA-SOTA!!
CLINK
CLINK
CHECK THIS OUT!
I CAN EVEN *PEE* WITH IT ON!
TRULY AMAZING!
HEY, AYANO! WE PULLED IT OFF!
OH...
Haah...
YEAH ...?
Haah...
?

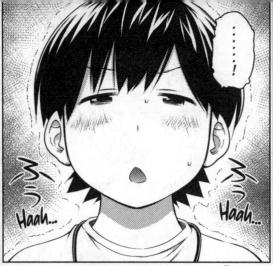

......!

Haah... Haah...

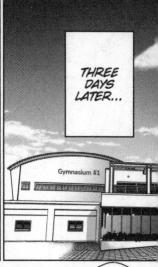

THREE DAYS LATER...

Gymnasium #1

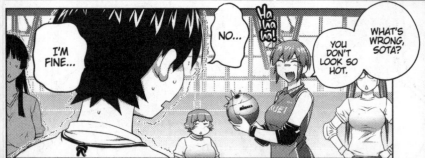

I'M FINE...

NO...

Ha ha ho!

YOU DON'T LOOK SO HOT.

WHAT'S WRONG, SOTA?

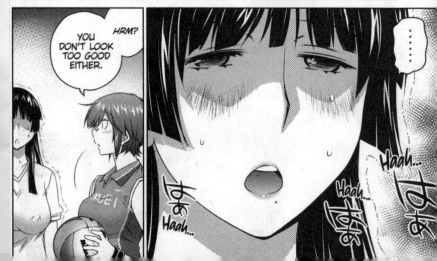

YOU DON'T LOOK TOO GOOD EITHER.

HRM?

......

Haah...

Haah... Haah... Haah...

WELL, YOU SEE...
I...
WANTED TO KNOW WHAT IT WAS LIKE...
CLINK
CLINK

CLINK
CLINK

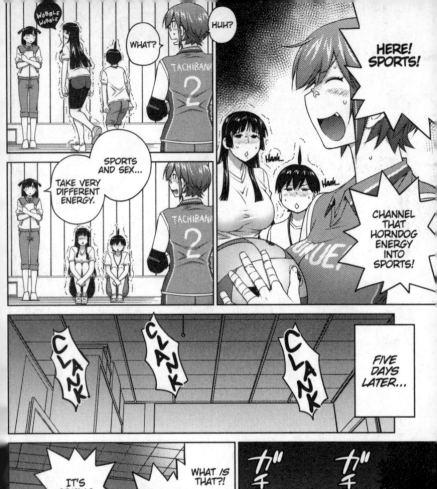

WOBBLE WOBBLE

WHAT?

HUH?

TACHIBANA 2

HERE! SPORTS!

SPORTS AND SEX...

TAKE VERY DIFFERENT ENERGY.

TACHIBANA 2

Haah...

Haah...

INOUE!

CHANNEL THAT HORNDOG ENERGY INTO SPORTS!

CLANK

CLANK

CLANK

FIVE DAYS LATER...

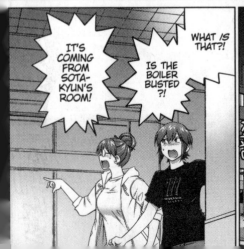

IT'S COMING FROM SOTA-KYUN'S ROOM!

IS THE BOILER BUSTED?!

WHAT *IS* THAT?!

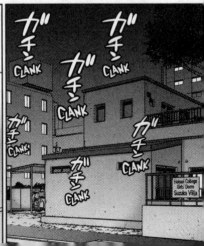

ガチン CLANK

ガチン CLANK

ガチン CLANK

ガチン CLANK

ガチン CLANK

ガチン CLANK

ガチン CLANK

Hakuei College Girls Dorm Suzuka Villa

INSIDE THEY FOUND TWO MISERABLE HUMAN BEINGS...
AAAAH!
OW! OW!
AAAAAH!
ガチン
CLANK
ガチン
CLANK
THAT HURTS!
BANGING THEIR CHASTITY BELTS TOGETHER.
CLANK
ガチン
ガチン
CLANK
ガチン
CLANK
CLANK
ガチン
THEY'RE ACTING LIKE TWO WILD ANIMALS LOCKED IN A CAGE...
I CAN'T HELP BUT FEEL SORRY FOR THEM...
ガチン
CLANK
YEAH...

ENOUGH ALREADY. HERE...
I'LL SET YOU FREE.
JINGLE
WAIT.
YOU PUT THAT BELT ON YOURSELF, RIGHT?
YOU COULD TAKE IT OFF ANYTIME YOU WANTED!
Haah!
Haah!
YEAH...
BUT I LOST THE KEY...
My room's a disaster area...

SHLCK

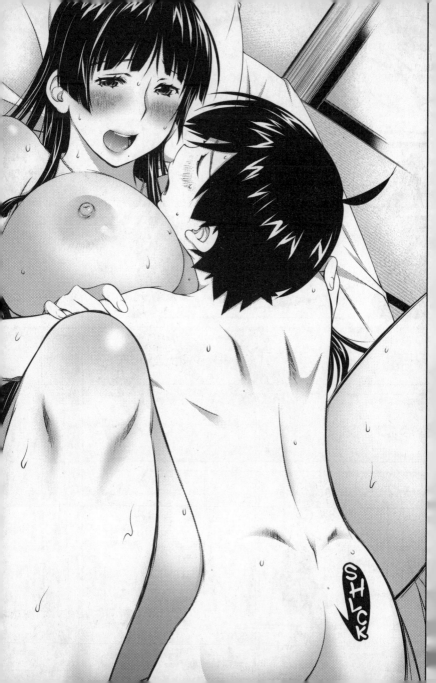

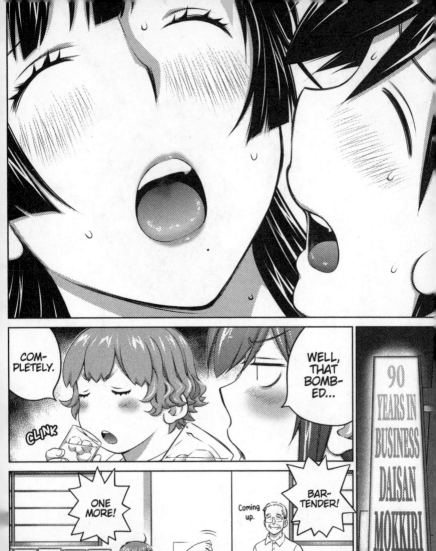

WELL, THAT BOMB-ED...

COM-PLETELY.

CLINK

ONE MORE!

Coming up.

BAR-TENDER!

90 YEARS IN BUSINESS DAISAN MOKKIRI CENTER

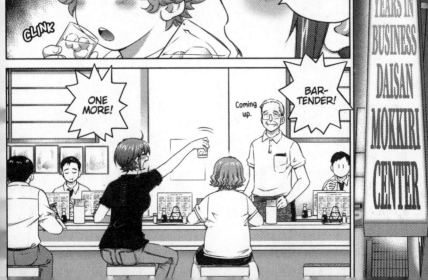

DO YOU LIKE BIG GIRLS?

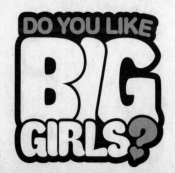

DO YOU LIKE BIG GIRLS?

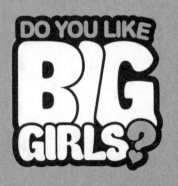

THE PRACTICE MATCH BETWEEN HOKUEI AND HOKUGAKUEN STARTS NOW!
PLAY HARD BUT FAIR!
THWACK
BMP
HOKUEI
WHAM
STAY IN YOUR LANE, ACE.
S...
SOR-RY...

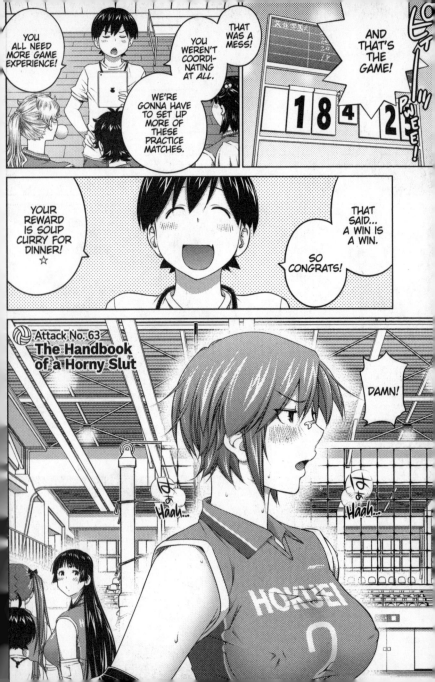

YOU ALL NEED MORE GAME EXPERIENCE!

YOU WEREN'T COORDINATING AT ALL.

THAT WAS A MESS!

WE'RE GONNA HAVE TO SET UP MORE OF THESE PRACTICE MATCHES.

AND THAT'S THE GAME!

18 4 2

PWEE!

YOUR REWARD IS SOUP CURRY FOR DINNER! ☆

THAT SAID... A WIN IS A WIN.

SO CONGRATS!

Attack No. 63
The Handbook of a Horny Slut

DAMN!

Haah...

Haah...

HOKUEI

2

VROOOM
KAORU SEEMS UPSET...
CRUNCH
CRUNCH
WHISPER
WHISPER
CLINK
CLINK
CLINK
CLINK
CLINK

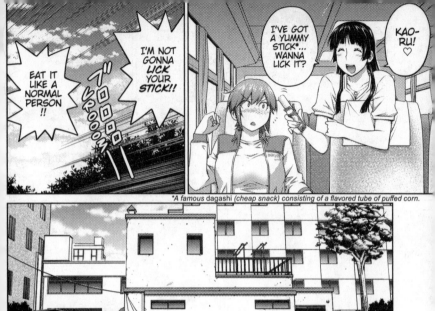

*A famous dagashi (cheap snack) consisting of a flavored tube of puffed corn.

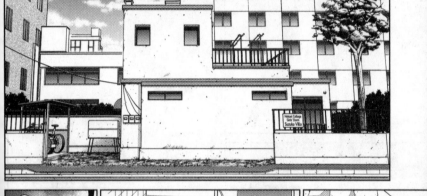

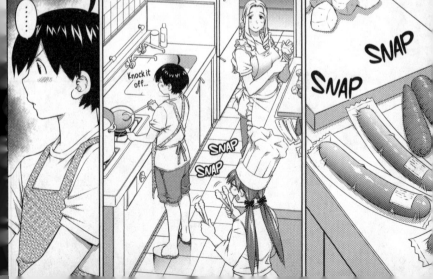

SOTA'S A DEDICATED COOK.
BEING A CHEF IS HIS DREAM JOB.
I'VE...
ALWAYS WANTED TO OPEN MY OWN SOUP CURRY SHOP.
I NEED TO PICK UP MORE SPICES FOR THE BROTH.
SAKURA-SAN, DON'T TOUCH ANYTHING, OKAY?
P-TMP
CREAK
DON'T. TOUCH. ANYTHING.
I HEARD YOU!
TMP
CRUNCH
CRUNCH
SCARY SUMMIT

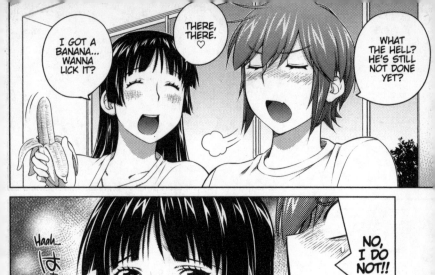

I GOT A BANANA... WANNA LICK IT?

THERE, THERE. ♡

WHAT THE HELL? HE'S STILL NOT DONE YET?

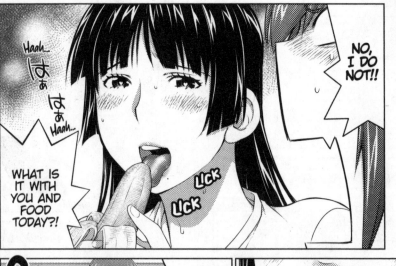

Haah... はぁ

はぁ Haah...

NO, I DO NOT!!

WHAT IS IT WITH YOU AND FOOD TODAY?!

LICK

LICK

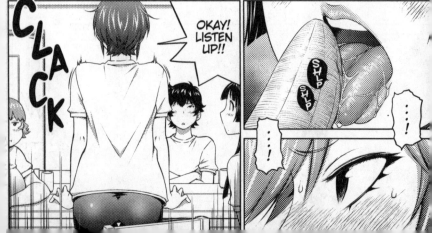

CLACK

OKAY! LISTEN UP!!

SHLP
SHLP

WHO HERE HAS... S...
SUCKED A DICK BEFORE...?
BLUSH
Yeppers!
Mm-hm.
I S-SEE...
You too, huh?
WHO DID WHAT?
SWOOP
OHO!
SEEING SOTA'S DICK THE OTHER DAY MUSTA LIT A FIRE INSIDE YOU.
Ha ha ha!
IT DID NOT!!
WHAT THE HELL'S WRONG WITH YOU?!
SNEAK

NIPPLE CHECK!!
GRAB!
SQUEEZE
HEY!
SQUEEZE
LET ME GO, YOU PERV!
THEY'RE ROCK HARD!
SHE'S TURNED ON BUT GOOD!
TWITCH
TWITCH
PINCH
PINCH
UH... WOW...
SHOVE

HERE. ♡
IT'S CLOSE TO THE REAL THING. ♡
SHLUP

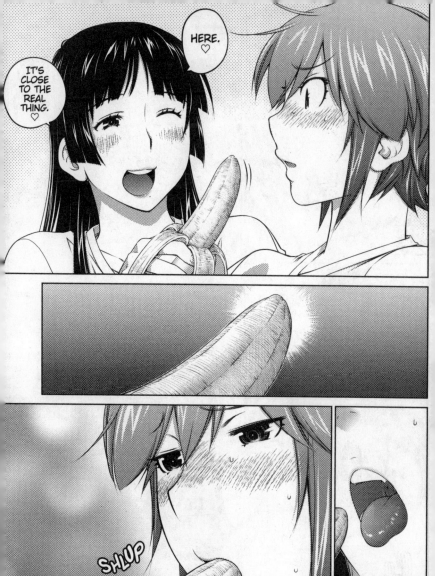

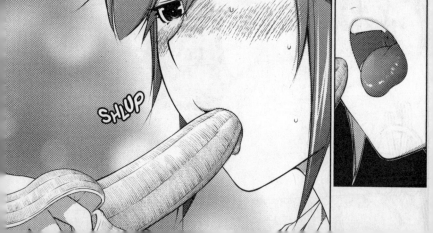

TREMBLE
SHLP
SHLP
TREMBLE
Mm!
Mmph!
HUH?
IS HER MOUTH THAT SENSI-TIVE?
SERI-OUSLY?
TREMBLE
TREMBLE

I KNOW...
VERY WELL HOW SENSITIVE IT IS. ♡
ガ
ぶ
CHOMP!
IT'S NOT SENSITIVE AT ALL!
I FOUND SOMETHING BETTER WE CAN USE!
Ptooie!
Tee hee!
EXTRA-THICK SAU-SAGES!

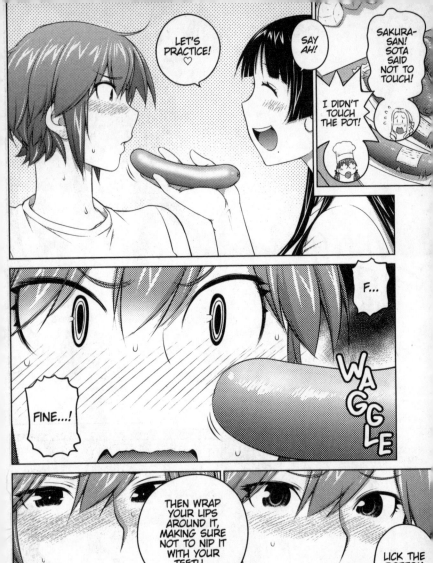

LET'S PRACTICE! ♥

SAY AH!

SAKURA-SAN! SOTA SAID NOT TO TOUCH!

I DIDN'T TOUCH THE POT!

F...

FINE...!

WAGGLE

THEN WRAP YOUR LIPS AROUND IT, MAKING SURE NOT TO NIP IT WITH YOUR TEETH...

SHURP

LICK THE BOTTOM FIRST.

LAP

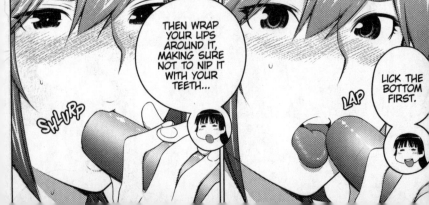

MM!
SHLUP
SHLUP
MMM!
SHLUP
Haah...
NOW...
I'M GONNA ...
Haah...
PUSH IT IN A LITTLE DEEPER.
TREMBLE TREMBLE
Haah...

JUFT A WI'L... MOWW. ♡
SHLURP
!
Mnph!
GULP
MNPH!
Mm!
MM!
Huff!
MMM!
Huff!
TREMBLE
GULP
MNPH!!
TREMBLES

TWITCH
GAG
WOBBLE
SHUDDER
GULP
GAGGG
Mngh!
CRASH!
ガタッ

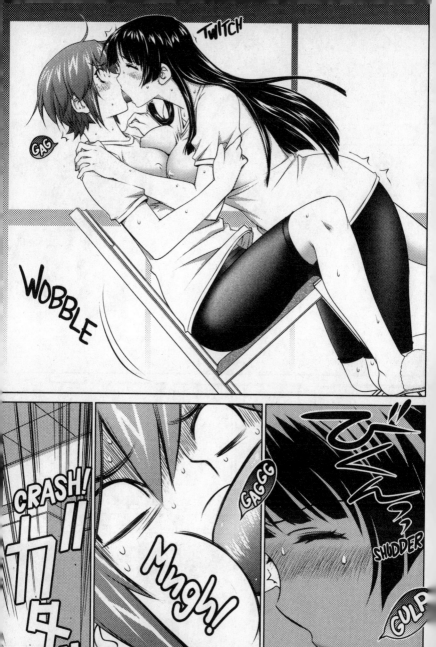

TREMBLE
DRIIP
TREMBLE
TWITCH
TWITCH
BLEEEH!
I'M BACK!
TREMBLE~
BLEEEH!
UM.
WHAT'S GOING ON?
IN THE END, I DIDN'T GET ANY DINNER.
MAINLY BECAUSE SOTA WAS SUPER PISSED AT WIDDLE OL' ME...

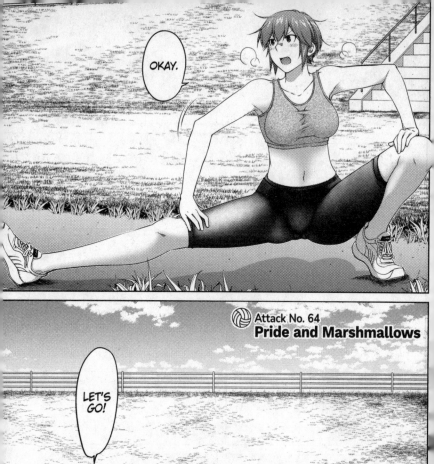

OKAY.

Attack No. 64
Pride and Marshmallows

LET'S GO!

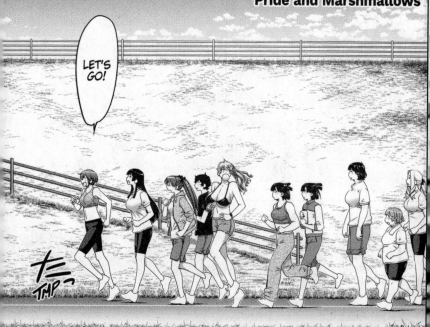

Haah! はぁっ
Haah! はぁっ
Haah! はぁっ
Haah! はぁっ
Haah! はぁっ
Haah! はぁっ
Haah!
Haah!
Mmm!
Haah!
Haah!
Haah!
Huff!
Huff!
Haah!
Haah!
Haah!
HUH?
WHERE'S MOMOMI?
SHE WENT BACK.
SAID SHE WASN'T FEELING IT.
Haah!
Haah!
Huh?
IS SHE SICK?
NOPE.
MORE LIKE SHE FELT OUR MORNING JOG WAS A WASTE OF TIME...
Haah!
Haah!
UH...
I'M GONNA HEAD BACK.
Haah!
Haah!
WHY DIDN'T YOU SAY SOMETHING?! YOU'RE THE *CAPTAIN!*
Here.
I MEAN...
Thanks.

Girls' Dorm
Suzuka Villa
ジャー
SIZZLE
......
TRY AND LEAVE SOME FOR THE REST OF US, HUH?
MUNCH
MUNCH
じゅわぁぁぁ
SIZZZZLE
......
HEY...
もっしゃ
MUNCH
もっしゃ
MUNCH
もっしゃ
MUNCH
MUNCH
YOUR GIRLFRIEND'S OKAY WITH THIS?
WH-- ?!
WHAT ?!

WELL...
I LIKE...
THE CAPTAIN, BUT...
WE'RE KINDA...
ON A BREAK RIGHT NOW, I GUESS...
......
UH-HUH?
MUNCH
HIII!
SHUFFLE
SHUFFLE
STOMP
AHA!
THERE YOU ARE!

WELCOME BACK!
UH.
HEY.
LISTEN!
YOU CAN'T JUST TAKE OFF LIKE THAT!
UH-HUH.
SURE.
CREAK
I WASN'T DOING ANYTHING, SO DON'T GET ALL BENT OUT OF SHAPE...
UPCHUCK ACE.
UPCH-- WHAT?!!

ON THAT NOTE...
I'M TIRED, SO I'M GONNA TAKE A NAP.
WHAT ABOUT BREAK-FAST?
I ATE WHAT I NEEDED TO ALREADY.
SOMEONE NEEDS TO SET HER STRAIGHT!
NOT IT!
IF SHE GETS UPSET, SHE MIGHT QUIT, SO...
SHEESH!
THESE FORMER YOUTH STARS ARE ALL EGO!
SHE'S REALLY CHECKED OUT.
WE'RE BOTH FIRST-YEARS, SO I'M SURE SHE'D LISTEN TO ME!
DOUBT IT.
YANK

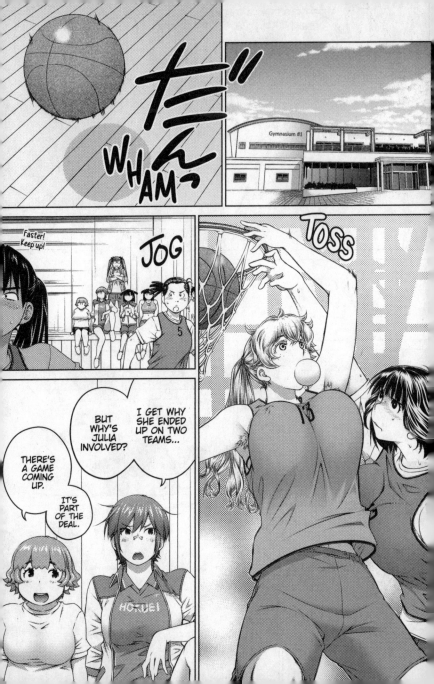

WHAM

Gymnasium #1

JOG

Faster! Keep up!

TOSS

BUT WHY'S JULIA INVOLVED?

I GET WHY SHE ENDED UP ON TWO TEAMS...

THERE'S A GAME COMING UP.

IT'S PART OF THE DEAL.

HOKUEI

ダン
DRIBBLE
ダン
DRIBBLE
WOW.
WENT RIGHT PAST HER.
Easily.
MOMO'S TOO HEAVY...
TOSS

FWO OO OO OSH
HEY... THAT MOVE YOU USED EARLIER.
COULD YOU SHOW ME HOW TO DO IT?
WOW!
HUH?
THEY'RE *BOTH* INVERTED!
WHAT ?!
WE'RE TWINS! ♡

I'M MAKING CHEESE-STUFFED HAMBURGER TONIGHT!
Hokuei College Girls' Dorm Suzuka Villa
UM... MOMOMI-CHAN...
PASS.
ON A DIET?
YOU SHOULD AT LEAST SIT WITH US.
GRRR.
YOU'RE THE ONE WHO COULD REALLY STAND TO SKIP A FEW MEALS...
CHEESE-STUFFED CAPTAIN.
SNAP

WOW.
THAT'S RICH COMING FROM THE STAY-PUFT MARSHMALLOW MAN'S JAPANESE COUSIN.
RAWR!
YOU COULD BE HIS STUNT DOUBLE!
SMIRK
FINE.
I'M STARTING A NEW HARDCORE WORKOUT TOMORROW ...
CARE TO JOIN ME, HAMBURGER HELPER?
Y-YOU'RE ON!
I'll fry her sunny-side up.

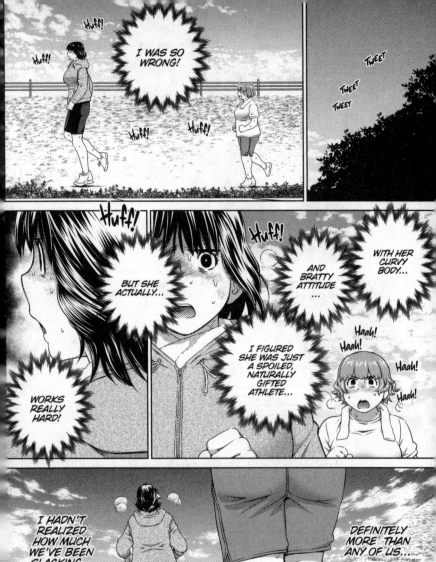

I WAS SO WRONG!

BUT SHE ACTUALLY...

AND BRATTY ATTITUDE...

WITH HER CURVY BODY...

I FIGURED SHE WAS JUST A SPOILED, NATURALLY GIFTED ATHLETE...

WORKS REALLY HARD!

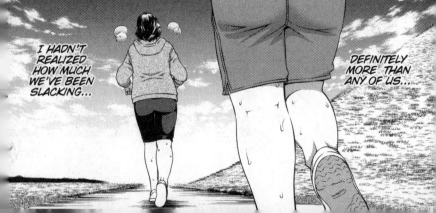

I HADN'T REALIZED HOW MUCH WE'VE BEEN SLACKING...

DEFINITELY MORE THAN ANY OF US...

COME TO THINK OF IT...
THOSE MORNING JOGS I STARTED DOING WITH SOTA-KUN...
DIDN'T LAST VERY LONG...
Huff!
Huff!
Huff!
Huff!
Huff!
Huff!
Haah!
Haa
SQUEAK
Haah!
I REFUSE...
TO LET TACHIBANA KAORU WIN.
Huff!
Huff!
Huff!
Huff!
Huff!
Huff!
SHE REALLY PISSES ME OFF.
AND THAT'S WHY...
I DON'T WANT YOU TO LET HER WIN EITHER.
Huff!
Huff!
Huff!

Haah!
Haah!
SHE CAN FUCK RIGHT OFF.
HA HA HA!
SHE IS PRETTY IRRITATING!
Haah!
Haah!
ATCHOO!
GOT A COLD?
BRUSH
BRUSH
BRUSH
BRUSH
BRUSH
BRUSH
OKAY!
TIME TO BRING THIS TO A BOIL!
A BOIL?
ARE YOU A POT OF STEW?
I'll show you who's stew.

SLIM
HOKUEI
WHOA! YOU LOOK SO DIFFER-ENT!
OOH!
OOOH!
SHOOF
SHOOF
STOP OGLING HER!
BONK
Hahahahaha!
?
HOKUEI

Hokuei College Girls' Dorm Suzuka Villa
71.3 kg
I ONLY LOST ONE KILOGRAM...
TREMBLE
TREMBLE
WHY CAN'T I SHAKE THIS WEIGHT?

DO YOU LIKE BIG GIRLS?

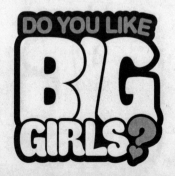

DO YOU LIKE BIG GIRLS?

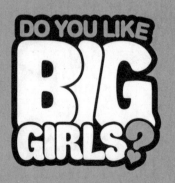

SHOOF
Ack!
DRIBBLE
DASH
HEY!
DID Y'ALL FORGET WHAT TEAM WE ARE?!
Crap!
Ha ha ha!

SQUEAK
WHERE'S THE CAP-TAIN?
ABOUT TO GO FOR A JOG.
HEY, CAPTAIN...
WANT SOME COMPANY?
......
I'M GOOD.

Attack No. 65
Say My Name

Huff!
Huff!
Huff!
Huff!
Huff!
Huff!
Huff!
はっ
Huff!
HE'S GOT SOME NERVE!
はっ
Huff!
はっ
Huff!
ASKING IF I WANT COMPANY!
はっ
Huff!
WHAT A DUMB THING TO ASK!
FUCK THAT!

SPARKLE
"LET'S GO FOR A JOG TOGETHER!"
THUMBS UP
THAT'S HOW YOU DO IT!
TURN
Haah!
Haah!
Haah!
Haah!
CHUG
CHUG
CHUG
CHUG
CHUG
CHUG
MOMOMI-CHAN REALLY IS SOMETHING...
BUT THEN, SHE *WAS* A STAR.
Sigh...
Hokkai Melon Cream Soda

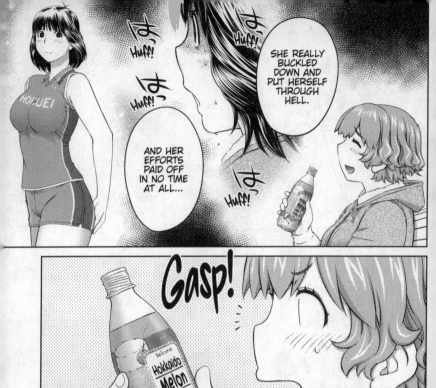

SHE REALLY BUCKLED DOWN AND PUT HERSELF THROUGH HELL.

AND HER EFFORTS PAID OFF IN NO TIME AT ALL...

は Huff!

は Huff!

は Huff!

は Huff!

Gasp!

Sakanna
Hokkaido
Melon

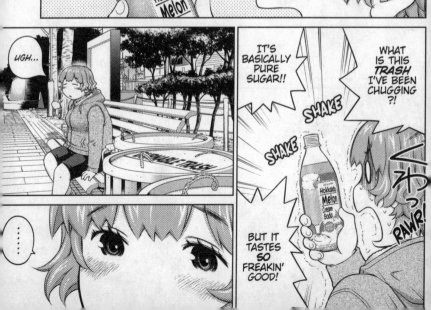

UGH...

DOUBLE TRASH

IT'S BASICALLY PURE SUGAR!!

WHAT IS THIS *TRASH* I'VE BEEN CHUGGING?!

SHAKE

SHAKE

Sakanna
Hokkaido
Melon
Cream
Soda

RAWR!

BUT IT TASTES SO FREAKIN' GOOD!

. . . . .

THE FACT IS...
HE DOESN'T ACTUALLY LIKE ME.
AND HE'S SAID AS MUCH...
AND YET A PART OF ME...
REFUSED TO BELIEVE IT.

Gymnasium #1
WHY ARE THOSE TWO...
SUDDENLY BEST FRIENDS?
DRIBBLE
DRIBBLE
WE'RE INVERTED-NIPPLE TWINS! ♡
ば
Ta-daaa!
YOU... SURE ARE...

Hokuei College Girls' Dorm Suzuka Villa
I MADE RAMEN SALAD FOR DINNER!
UM...
PASS.
BUT RAMEN SALAD IS HEALTHY, SO MAYBE...
I'M FINE.
CRUNCH

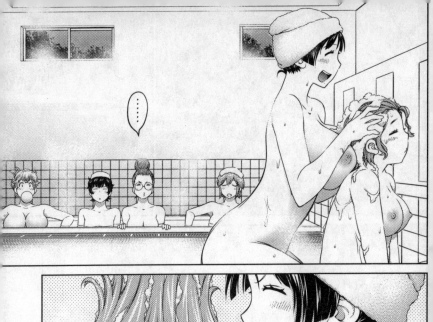

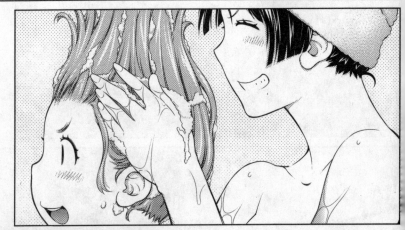

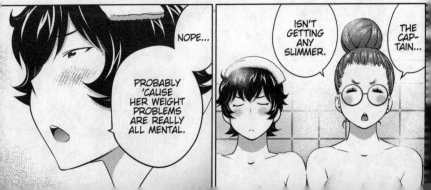

NOPE...

PROBABLY 'CAUSE HER WEIGHT PROBLEMS ARE REALLY ALL MENTAL.

ISN'T GETTING ANY SLIMMER.

THE CAP-TAIN...

CREAK
SOTA ...
SOTA ...
HEY, SHORTY...
THE YOUNGER OF THE DUM-DUM SIBLINGS.
MM...

HEY!
Nyam
Nyam
SUUUUUUUCK
SHOOP
QUIT IT!
THAT'S NOT WHY I'M HERE...!
SHLURP
RUSTLE
RUSTLE
RUSTLE
RUSTLE

MUNCH
MUNCH
MUNCH
MUNCH
MUNCH
MUNCH
UH...
CAP-TAIN?
OH...
HUH...?

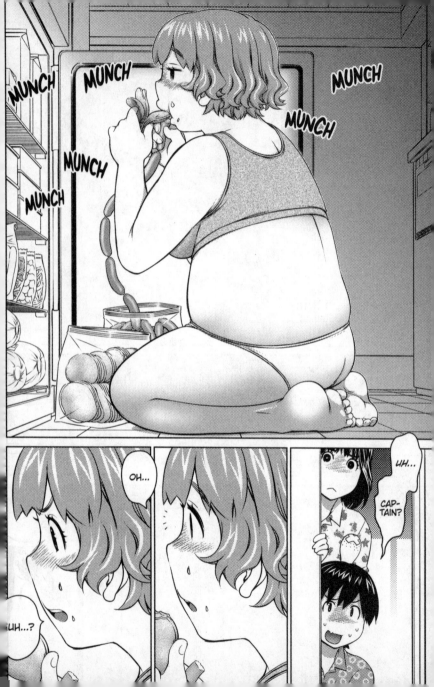

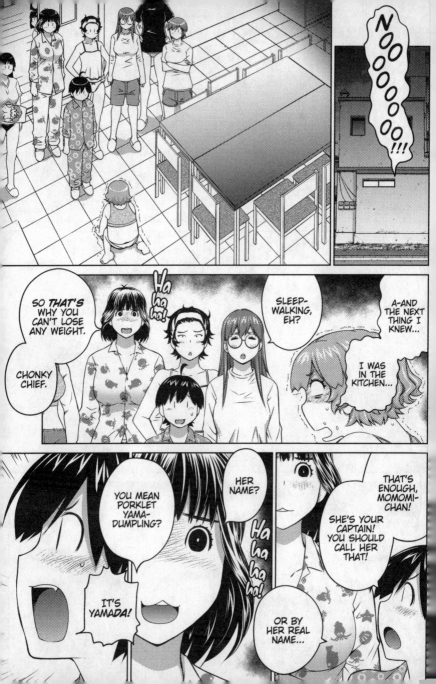

NOOOOOOOO!!!

SO *THAT'S* WHY YOU CAN'T LOSE ANY WEIGHT.

CHONKY CHIEF.

Ha ha ha!

SLEEP-WALKING, EH?

A-AND THE NEXT THING I KNEW...

I WAS IN THE KITCHEN...

YOU MEAN PORKLET YAMA-DUMPLING?

HER NAME?

Ha ha ha!

IT'S YAMADA!

THAT'S ENOUGH, MOMOMI-CHAN!

SHE'S YOUR CAPTAIN! YOU SHOULD CALL HER THAT!

OR BY HER REAL NAME...

YAMADA SATSUKI-CHAN!
SOTA...
MY NAME'S SANAE.

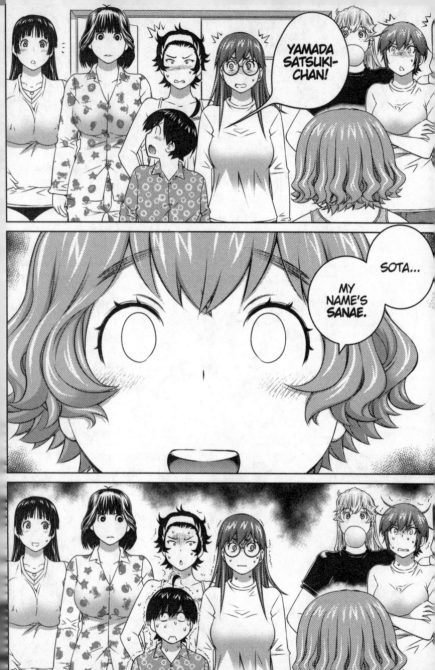

WELL.
TIME FOR BED.
SLAM
WELL, *THAT* WAS MORTI-FYING!
ARE YOU *FOR REAL?!*
HOW COULD YOU *BLANK* ON THE NAME OF YOUR OWN *GIRLFRIEND?!*
GO APOLOGIZE. NOW.
THIS GOES WAY PAST APOLOGIES...

WHAM!
NEE...
CHAN...
GO APOLO-GIZE!!
RIGHT NOW!

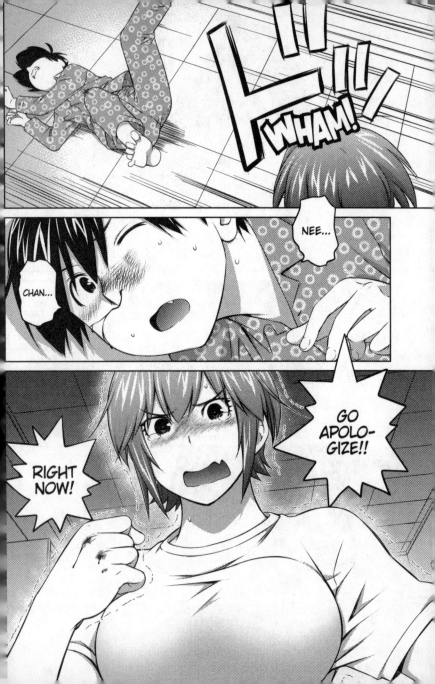

DO YOU LIKE BIG GIRLS?

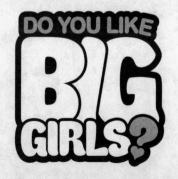

DO YOU LIKE BIG GIRLS?

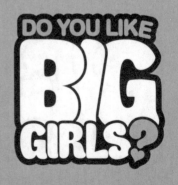

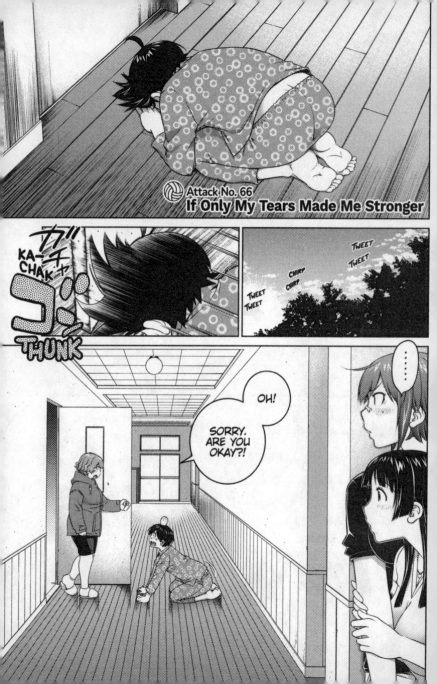

Attack No. 66
If Only My Tears Made Me Stronger

KA-
CHAK

THUNK

TWEET
TWEET

CHIRP
CHIRP

TWEET
TWEET

OH!

SORRY.
ARE YOU
OKAY?!

SO, CAPTAIN...
I MEAN, SANAE-SAN.
"CAPTAIN" IS FINE.
OH.
RIGHT.
TWEET
TWEET
THIS IS POINTLESS.
CHIRP
CHIRP
CHIRP
I'M GOING BACK TO BED.
C-CAPTAIN?
......

THWACK!
ゴロゴロ ROLL ROLL
ダッ STOMP
HI-YAH!
HEY, CAPTAIN. ABOUT YESTERDAY...
Haah!
I ALREADY TOLD YOU, EVERYTHING'S FINE!
SO QUIT BRINGING IT UP!
Haah!
TOSS ME ONE MORE!

I'M STARVING!
SSH!
HOW ABOUT SOME MEAT?
I HAVEN'T GONE OUT FOR YAKINIKU IN AGES!
OH, RIGHT. WHAT IF SOTA-KUN ALREADY STARTED MAKING DINNER?
UH... BUT...
Your diet...
CAN YOU CHECK, KAORU?
UH... SURE...

SO...
HE HASN'T STARTED YET...
GREAT!
THEN HOW ABOUT I TAKE US ALL OUT FOR YAKINIKU TONIGHT! ♡
SURE...

SO YUMMY!!! ♡
IT MELTS IN MY MOUTH! ♡♡
IT'S LIKE MY MIND'S MELTING, TOO! ♡♡♡
SQUEAK
WHEW!
IT'S TOO BAD SOTA-KUN COULDN'T JOIN US!
UH... YEP...
SHE'S FORCING IT, RIGHT?
VERY MUCH SO...
MUNCH MUNCH
CAP-TAIN!
I'M SO SORRY MY BROTH-ER'S...
BOW
A FRIGGIN' DUMMY!!

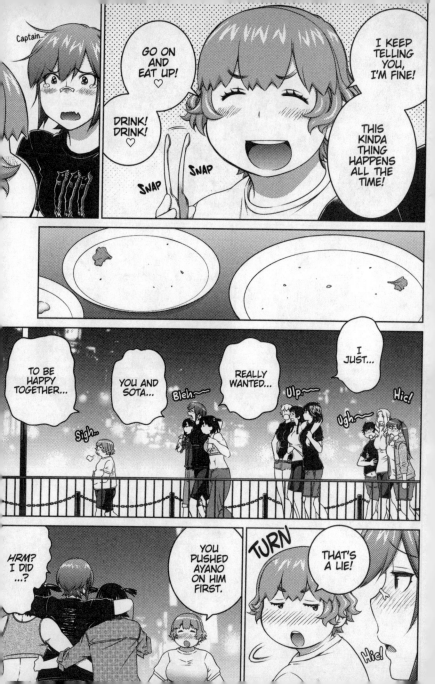

Captain...

GO ON AND EAT UP! ♥

DRINK! DRINK! ♥

SNAP SNAP SNAP

I KEEP TELLING YOU, I'M FINE!

THIS KINDA THING HAPPENS ALL THE TIME!

TO BE HAPPY TOGETHER...

YOU AND SOTA...

Sigh...

Bleh~

REALLY WANTED...

Ulp~

I JUST...

Ugh~

Hic!

HRM? I DID ...?

YOU PUSHED AYANO ON HIM FIRST.

TURN

THAT'S A LIE!

Hic!

WELL.
TO BE FAIR, HE *HAS* FUCKED EVERYONE ON THE TEAM.
NOT ME.
WHAT'S HIS DEAL...?
......
I JUST WANT...
SOTA TO BE HAPPY...
BUT THAT'S...
NOT SOMETHING I CAN HELP HIM WITH...

FLING—
FLING—
YOU'RE NOT DRUNK, MOMOMI.
WANNA TOUCH MY BOOBS?
JIGGLE
NO.
だんっ
THWACK!

Gymnasium #1
UM...
HEY...
SLIM

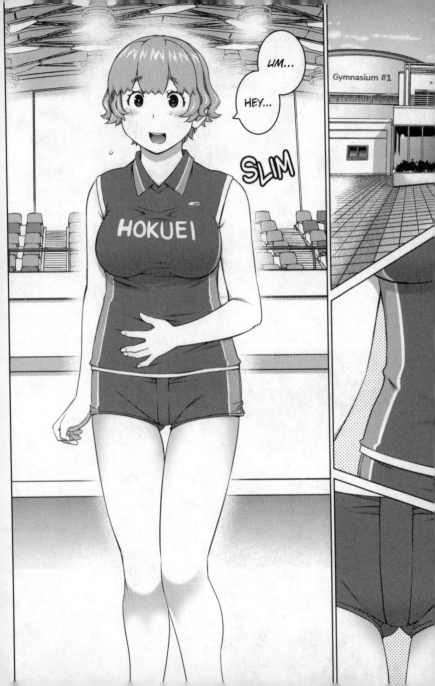

WHA? YOUR DIET HASN'T CHANGED, SO...
H... HOW'D YOU DO IT?
OH.
RIGHT.
I FINALLY...
GAVE UP ON HIM...
DRIP

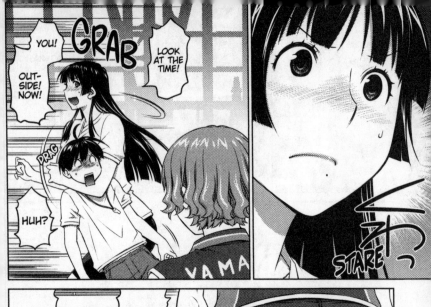

YOU!

OUT-SIDE! NOW!

GRAB

LOOK AT THE TIME!

DRAG

HUH?

STARE

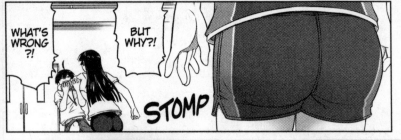

WHAT'S WRONG?!

BUT WHY?!

STOMP

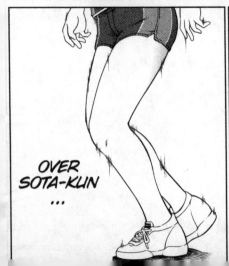

OVER SOTA-KUN ...

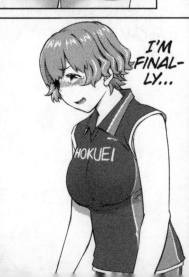

I'M FINAL-LY...

GRAB
ZERO TO THREE.
THE SCORE WAS ZERO TO THREE.
IN THE SPRING HIGH SCHOOL VOLLEYBALL FINALS.

WE'D PRACTICED HARD...
AND PLAYED EVEN HARDER.
AND YET IT STILL WASN'T ENOUGH.
DESPITE EVERY-THING...
WE ENDED UP IN SECOND PLACE.
IN THAT MOMENT, I NEVER WANTED TO PLAY AGAIN.
BUT...
THAT'S WHEN I SAW THE ELDER DUM-DUM SIBLING.
AND I KNEW THERE WAS NO WAY I WAS GONNA LET HER WIN.
WHICH IS WHY...
IF YOU THINK FOR ONE SECOND I'M GONNA LET YOU BREAK DOWN AND QUIT...
YOU'RE WRONG.

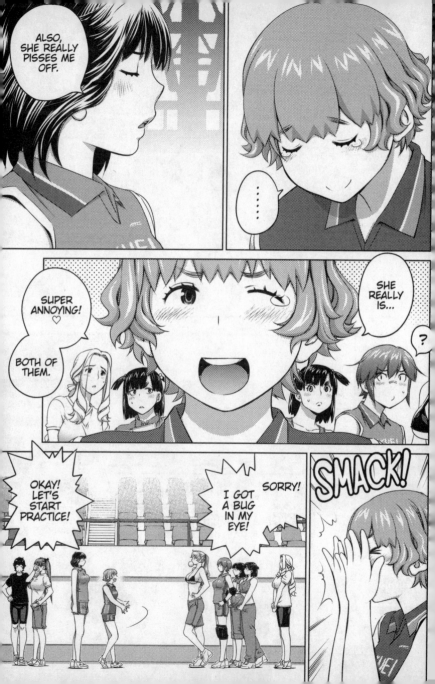

ALSO, SHE REALLY PISSES ME OFF.

......

SUPER ANNOYING! ♡

SHE REALLY IS...

BOTH OF THEM.

?

OKAY! LET'S START PRACTICE!

I GOT A BUG IN MY EYE!

SORRY!

SMACK!

HUG
HEY, AYANO-SAN. WHY DID WE GO FOR A WALK AGAIN?
CALL IT FEMALE INTUITION.
Or something.
SQUISH
HEY!
LOOK OVER THERE! A DICK CLOUD! ♡
EH. DO YOU SEE ANY BOOB CLOUDS?

DO YOU LIKE BIG GIRLS?

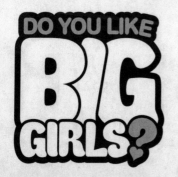

DO YOU LIKE BIG GIRLS?

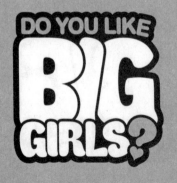

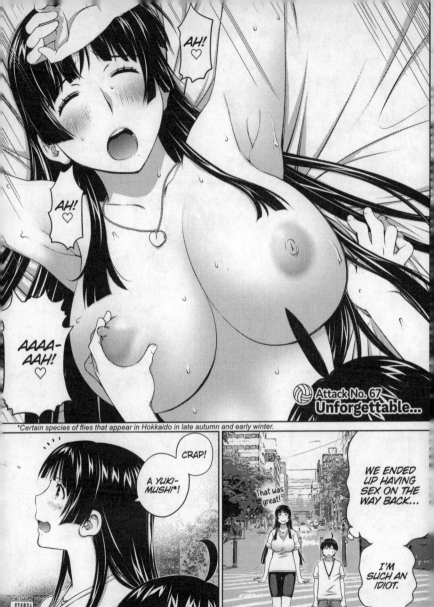

AH! ♥

AH! ♥

AAAA-AAH! ♥

**Attack No. 67
Unforgettable...**

*Certain species of flies that appear in Hokkaido in late autumn and early winter.

CRAP!

A YUKI-MUSHI*!

That was great!

WE ENDED UP HAVING SEX ON THE WAY BACK...

I'M SUCH AN IDIOT.

Hokusei College
Girls' Dorm
Suzuka Villa
WE'RE HOME.
.....
Welcome back.
I SAW A YUKI-MUSHI!
UGH! WINTER ALREADY?
UH...
HEY...

UM... HERE.
I GOT YOU SOMETHING.
SNIFF
SNIFF
......
YOU REEK OF HOTEL SOAP.
Eep!
JERK
TREMBLE
TREMBLE
AYANO!!
TREMBLE
TREMBLE
DID YOU GUYS FUCK?
I'm sorry!
......

WELL.
IT'S FINE.
ACTUALLY, I'M GRATEFUL.
AYANO GOT SOTA-KUN OUT OF THERE FOR ME.
I APPRE-CIATE IT.
IF HE'D SEEN ME IN THAT STATE...
THAT WOULD'VE BEEN THE END FOR REAL.

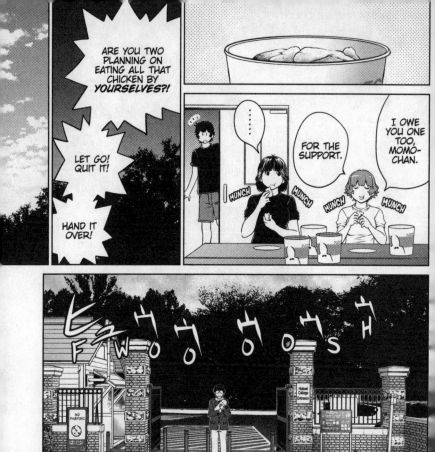

ARE YOU TWO PLANNING ON EATING ALL THAT CHICKEN BY **YOURSELVES?!**

LET GO! QUIT IT!

HAND IT OVER!

......

FOR THE SUPPORT.

I OWE YOU ONE TOO, MOMO-CHAN.

MUNCH

MUNCH

MUNCH

MUNCH

FWOOOOOSH

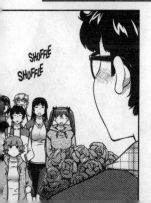

SHUFFLE

SHUFFLE

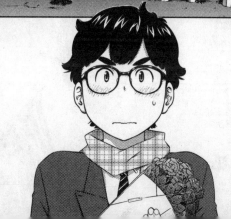

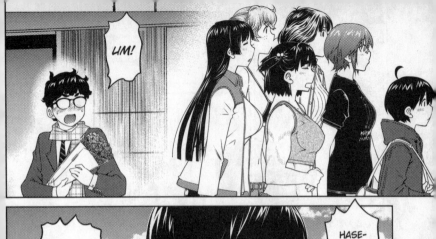

UM!

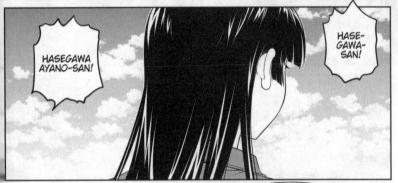

HASEGAWA AYANO-SAN!

HASE-GAWA-SAN!

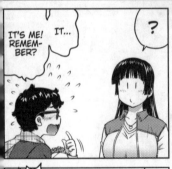

IT'S ME! REMEM-BER?

IT...

?

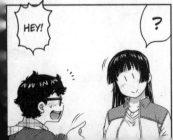

HEY!

?

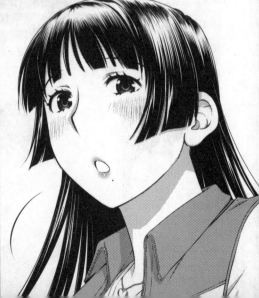

OH!
THAT'S THE LOCKET I GAVE YOU!
YOU'RE STILL WEARING IT!
JINGLE
YEP! ♡
UH... IS THAT THE ONE WITH THE PICTURE OF YOUR ...?
YUP ...
WHAT ?!
CLATTER
Y...
YOU'RE...
AYANO'S FIRST PART-NER?!
Fried Vegetable Gyoza with Rice 800 Yen
YANK
WELL... YES...
ON THAT NOTE! ♡
SEE YA! ♡
HEY! WAIT!

Huff!
Huff!
Huff!
Huff!
Huff!
Huff!
SO WAS THAT AYANO'S EX... BOYFRIEND?
NOT QUITE...
I DON'T THINK AYANO HAS BOYFRIENDS EXACTLY...

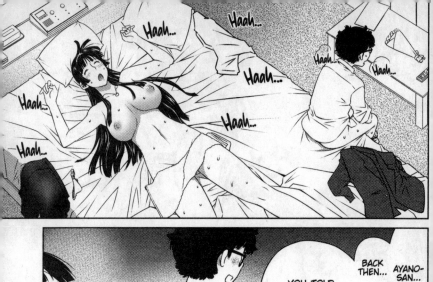

Haah... Haah... Haah... Haah... Haah... Haah... Haah... Haah...

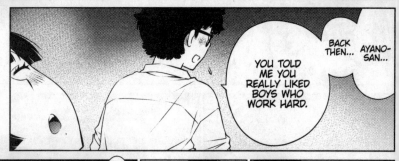

BACK THEN... AYANO-SAN... YOU TOLD ME YOU REALLY LIKED BOYS WHO WORK HARD.

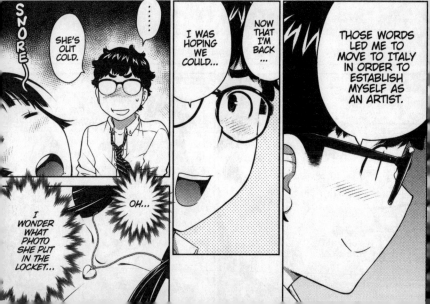

SNORE

....

SHE'S OUT COLD.

I WAS HOPING WE COULD...

NOW THAT I'M BACK...

THOSE WORDS LED ME TO MOVE TO ITALY IN ORDER TO ESTABLISH MYSELF AS AN ARTIST.

OH...

I WONDER WHAT PHOTO SHE PUT IN THE LOCKET...

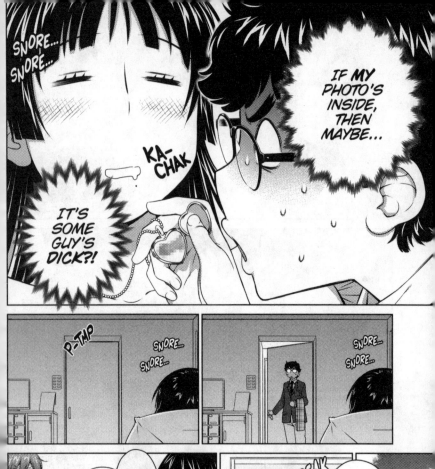

SNORE... SNORE...

KA-CHAK

IF MY PHOTO'S INSIDE, THEN MAYBE...

IT'S SOME GUY'S DICK?!

P-TAP

SNORE... SNORE...

SNORE... SNORE...

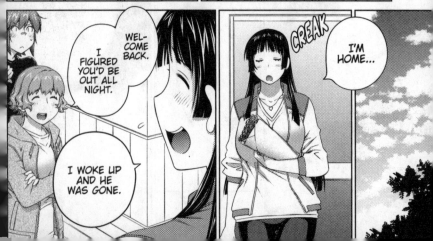

WEL-COME BACK.

I FIGURED YOU'D BE OUT ALL NIGHT.

I WOKE UP AND HE WAS GONE.

CREAK

I'M HOME...

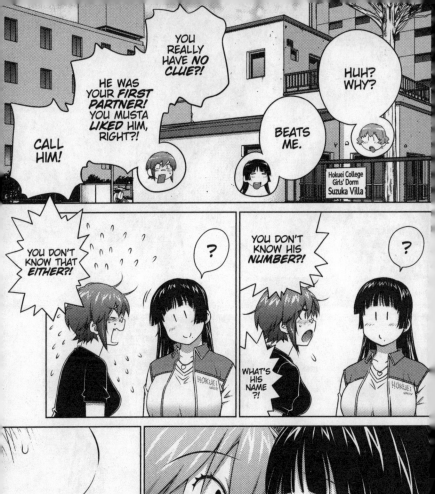

YOU REALLY HAVE *NO* CLUE?!

HE WAS YOUR *FIRST PARTNER!* YOU MUSTA *LIKED* HIM, RIGHT?!

CALL HIM!

HUH? WHY?

BEATS ME.

Hokuei College Girls' Dorm
Suzuka Villa

YOU DON'T KNOW THAT *EITHER?!*

?

YOU DON'T KNOW HIS *NUMBER?!*

WHAT'S HIS NAME?!

?

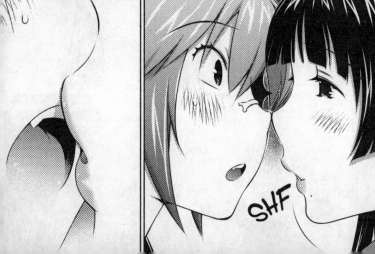

SHF

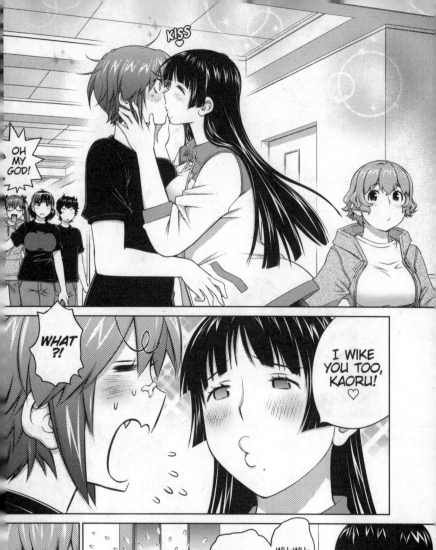

KISS

OH MY GOD!

I WIKE YOU TOO, KAORU! ♡

WHAT ?!

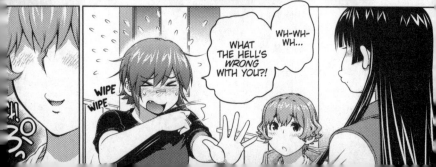

WIPE WIPE

WH-WH-WH...

WHAT THE HELL'S WRONG WITH YOU?!

ははははは
BWA HA HA HA!
AYANO! ♡
I CAN'T EVEN! ♡
Ha ha ha ha!
......
IT'S BEEN A WHILE...
SINCE I HEARD THE CAPTAIN LAUGH.
Mm-hm.
YEP! ♡

I JUST BAKED AN APPLE P--
I WIKE YOU TOO, CAPTAIN! ♡
P...
PIE...
SMOOCH
ST... STOP!
SQUISH
MM! ♡
OKAY!
AND ON THAT NOTE, LET'S EAT!
UH...
C-CAP-TAIN...
CUT THE PIE, SOTA-KUN!
COME ON, MOMOMI-CHAN! TAKE A SEAT!
NOW THEN!
BON APPETIT!!

DO YOU LIKE BIG GIRLS?

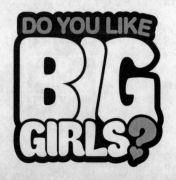

SEVEN SEAS' GHOST SHIP PRESENTS

DO YOU LIKE BIG GIRLS?

story and art by GORO AIZOME   VOLUME 7

TRANSLATION
Miki Z

ADAPTATION
Brett Hallahan

LETTERING
Cedric Macias

COVER DESIGN
Nicky Lim

LOGO DESIGN
George Panella

PROOFREADER
Leighanna DeRouen

COPY EDITOR
B. Lillian Martin

EDITOR
Nick Mamatas

PRODUCTION DESIGNER
George Panella

PRODUCTION MANAGER
Lissa Pattillo

PREPRESS TECHNICIAN
Melanie Ujimori
Jules Valera

EDITOR-IN-CHIEF
Julie Davis

ASSOCIATE PUBLISHER
Adam Arnold

PUBLISHER
Jason DeAngelis

OOKII ONNANOKO WA SUKI DESUKA? Volume 7
© 2021 GORO AIZOME
Originally published in Japan in 2021 by TAKESHOBO Co. LTD., Tokyo.
English translation rights arranged with TAKESHOBO Co. LTD., Tokyo,
through TOHAN CORPORATION, Tokyo.

Seven Seas press and purchase enquiries can be sent to Marketing Manager Lianne
Sentar at press@gomanga.com. Information regarding the distribution and purchase of
digital editions is available from Digital Manager CK Russell at digital@gomanga.com.

ISBN: 978-1-68579-538-2
Printed in Canada
First Printing: June 2023
10 9 8 7 6 5 4 3 2 1

//// READING DIRECTIONS ////

This book reads from *right to left*,
Japanese style. If this is your first time
reading manga, you start reading from
the top right panel on each page and
take it from there. If you get lost, just
follow the numbered diagram here.
It may seem backwards at first,
but you'll get the hang of it! Have fun!!

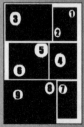

Follow us online: www.GhostShipManga.com